# The Adventures of Trooper Hayden and Skipper: Maine's First State Police K9 Unit

Written by:  Jennifer Deering

Illustrated by:  Sarah Deering

# DEDICATION

This book is dedicated to my dad for his bravery on the job and my mom for the sacrifices she made as the wife of a state trooper- and to both for their unending love and support.

Did you know that the Maine State Police did not always have a K9, or police dog, unit? Did you also know that the first dog trained as a Maine State Police K9 almost wasn't? I am that dog and this is my story.

**My Official Pedigree**

My name is Skipper. Actually, I come from some very fancy champion German blood-lines and have an equally fancy name, but I prefer to go by Skipper; it sounds tougher. I was born to a breeder in Skowhegan, Maine. When I was just a few months old, an elderly couple bought me and took me to their home.

    I spent most of my time with them tied to a tree outside. Not much of a life for a rambunctious pup like me! At 14 months old, I wasn't even house-trained. How embarrassing! One day, I growled at my owner lady (I don't even remember why) and before I knew it, I was back at the kennel! I wondered what would happen to me next.

At the same time that I was…um…between residences, there was a young State Trooper who had heard about the possibility of starting a K9 unit in Maine. This man, Trooper Dennis Hayden, grew up on a farm and was married with 2 young kids. He thought being a K9 handler would be fun. He was eating lunch one day when he heard about a dog that was available- and that dog was me!

Trooper Hayden drove to my new temporary residence and checked me out. I tried to look uninterested, but I really wanted to go to a forever home! After sizing me up, Trooper Hayden loaded me into the back of the police cruiser (Oh boy! Oh boy!) and drove me to his house to meet the family.

I got to laze around the house and play with kids for a long time. I quite liked this place! The kids were fun, the food was good, and I was actually allowed in the house…all the time! When Trooper Hayden went to work, I got to go with him….in the police car…with the sirens and blue lights! I was in doggy heaven!

After about 2 months of living it up as a part-time house pet and part-time riding partner, it was time for Trooper Hayden and me to go off to school. The only problem was that the closest K9 training school was in Connecticut. We were in school for 5 days and then off for 3. On our off days, we would go home to our family and rest. I missed my humans, but luckily I got to have my favorite with me all the time!

This is me with some of my classmates in 1980.

In later years, I helped train others. Here I am (in the driver's seat) with some of my trainees.

K9 training school was hard work! We trained eight to nine hours a day for twelve weeks before Trooper Hayden and I were certified to work patrol duty. In doggy years, that is…well…a really, really long time! We started out working on obedience. I had to learn to listen to Trooper Hayden and do what he asked. We were a great team, but sometimes I wanted to be the top dog. Trooper Hayden always let me know who was boss, though- and it wasn't me. He was nice about it and I always wanted to please him. There was nothing I liked better than some loving from my human and a few tosses of a ball.

After we learned a few simple tricks (like coming, sitting, fetching, heeling, and all that jazz), we got into the really fun stuff. We learned how to find things based on the smell that they give off. We trained to recover evidence that would have human smell on it, just in case a bad guy threw some out of a vehicle or something like that. It was hard work, but I was a hard worker with an amazing sniffer (that's nose in dog speak).

I learned how to go up ladders and down slides. That was fun! I also learned how to go across log bridges. That was scary stuff!

This was what it looked like when we were training for handler protection. Someone pretended to be a bad guy and dressed up in a big puffy suit that protected him from bites. This looks scary, but we had to know how to protect our humans! (Photo courtesy of the Maine State Police)

As the weeks went on, we also worked on what is called "handler protection." Trooper Hayden was my handler and I learned how to protect him. As it turns out, it was a lot more than just biting the bad guy! I was taught to bite only when needed and to protect my human at all times. I loved him, so that part was going to be easy! We also did building searches where I was taught to bite if someone was hiding in the building. That way, they couldn't hurt my human.

We trained in the day, in noisy areas, and at night. We went to all kinds of different areas. They took us to any place that might look like something we would encounter on the job (I, Skipper, was going to have a job! How exciting was that?). We had to know how to react to any situation that we might find ourselves in. They even shot guns in our direction. I was brave, though- and so was Trooper Hayden.

Trooper Hayden and I on graduation day

Receiving our diploma

It was official! I was a graduate!

After 12 weeks of practicing and practicing and practicing (and practicing), Trooper Hayden and I became a lean, mean crime-fighting machine. We went home to Maine and became the first official K9 unit the Maine State Police had ever had.

**We were a pretty tough looking team, don't you think?**

Trooper Hayden and I had many adventures together. I loved to ride in the cruiser and bark in his ear (which could explain why, later, he became a little hard of hearing), but I really liked to get out and do some work! I was bummed when he had to sit at the barracks and write reports.

### Hunt for missing inmates

About 150 state troopers, prison guards, sheri's' deputies and other officials combed the woods the Searsmont area on Saturday and Sunday, arching for two inmates missing from Maine State Prison since July 15. A police dog was shot and several officers were fired upon during the weekend incident. The inmates were spotted in a Searsmont blueberry field Saturday noon. (Story, Page One.) (NEWS Photo by T. J. Tremble.)

**That's Trooper Hayden and me on the left. We are heading out to search for the bad guys.**

One of our most famous adventures happened early on in our career and was what is now known in Maine as the Moody Mountain Manhunt. That was the biggest manhunt in the history of the state at the time. Many different agencies from across Maine were on the hunt for two scary guys who had escaped from the state prison. Using my amazing sniffer, I had tracked them down two different times over a three week period, but they kept getting away.

One day, after we had been working for hours, I picked up their scent again! I was on the trail, but the trail was rugged and temperatures were high. After a while, Trooper Hayden pulled me off because he was afraid I was going to collapse from heat exhaustion. I was tough as nails and liked a good challenge- but he was smart enough to know that I needed a break. Shortly after that, another police dog (named Ben) was shot by those meanies! (Don't worry, though, he was also tough as nails and survived!).

Later on that same day, in a driving rain, we were ready to try again. One of the people in charge wanted to bring in some bloodhounds because they didn't think I could track the bad guys in such heavy rain. Geez! How insulting! Trooper Hayden convinced him that we could do it- and we did! We snuck up on those bad guys and appeared out of nowhere like ghosts. Boy, were they surprised!

"You shot Skipper's buddy- and he is NOT happy," said Trooper Hayden as I kept my eyes on the men- and my teeth showing, for good measure!

Soon, they were arrested and brought back to jail. I got a lot of loving from my human after that one, and the Maine State Police K9 program got a lot of loving from everyone!

**The bad guys in handcuffs, ready to head back to jail. (Photo courtesy of the Maine State Police)**

We even got a commendation and a "Good Boy!"
from Colonel Allen Weeks for our help in catching those
bad guys!

Tr. Dennis R. Hayden
R.F.D. #1, Route 32
Vassalboro, ME  04989

Dear Trooper Hayden:

    I would like to take this opportunity to commend you
and Skipper for outstanding performance during the recent
prison escapee search in the Searsmont-Morrill area.

    On two occasions, your immediate response with Skipper
and accompanied by Warden Ford resulted in the successful
tracking of the wanted subjects and in their apprehension
in the latter case.

    I am fully cognizant of the fact that on August 5,
1981, you had already worked some eleven hours, yet you
responded at once to the request at Morrill and under ad-
verse tracking conditions, Skipper was able to trail the
subjects to their location.

    Your dedication and iniative during this assignment
has earned the Maine State Police and the K-9 unit the
respect and recognition of its counterparts in New England.

    You have every right to be proud of your professional
effectiveness and of Skipper; I am!

                                Sincerely,

                                COLONEL ALLAN H. WEEKS
                                Chief

AHW/slw

**This is what I looked like when that man made me mad! I could be pretty scary looking when I wanted to!**

A few years later, Trooper Hayden and I were on patrol again when he stopped a woman and a man because they were driving all crazy. As my human was talking to the woman driver and trying to keep her dog under control, I saw the man get out of the car and walk slowly around it toward him. The man was trying to sneak up behind my human. I knew something was not right. I jumped out of that car and knocked the man down. When I did, a large knife fell out of his hand. He was going to hurt my human! Oh, that made me mad! I stayed right on top of that man and was barking in his face while my human dealt with the crazy lady. Finally, more help arrived and both of the bad people were taken to jail. That was quite the adventure. I saved my human's life that day, for sure!

Some of my adventures were the result of some, shall we say, crazy driving on Trooper Hayden's part! That man did NOT like to lose a bad guy. One night, Trooper Hayden was showing a dispatcher (those are the guys who tell the police where to go over the radio) the tricks of the trade. It was late at night and I was snoozing in the back seat. Next thing I know, I was going head over tail, as we were crashing. Somehow, I ended up outside the cruiser and was sitting there watching as my human and his friend crawled out through the back window to safety. I have no idea what happened, but I do know that we got a new police car after that adventure!

Here is our car after the crash. For the record, wheels should never be pointing in this direction!

Some of my favorite times were when we found kids who were lost in the woods. I could be a tough guy, but I was a big softie when it came to kids. We once found an 8 year old who had been lost for hours in the woods. It was night time and several people were looking for the boy. After three hours, I was able to track him down, several miles from his home.

Another time, I tracked a two year old who got lost in the woods wearing only a t-shirt and diaper! I found him about a mile from his house. As you can imagine, the mom was quite happy with us! Those stories with the happy endings were always my favorite!

Over time, Trooper Hayden and I developed quite a tight bond; I was not going to let anything happen to him. I was trained early on to jump into the front seat with the window down when Trooper Hayden would get out of the car for a traffic stop. I was always watching to be sure he was safe. After all, being a police officer is a dangerous job! Eventually, I decided that at night, I would jump out of the cruiser, circle around the bad guy's car to let him know I was there, and then jump back in the cruiser to watch. That was my own thing; I wasn't trained to do that. Just like Trooper Hayden, I loved my job and was always looking to do it better.

This is kind of what our cruiser looked like when I was done. Oops! My bad!

One time, Trooper Hayden forgot to put his window down when he got out to chat with a bad guy. I had my nose glued to the window watching them. Suddenly, the bad guy took off running- and so did Trooper Hayden! I was frantic! I barked and scratched and tore around that car looking for a way out to help my human. After what seemed like forever, he came back with the bad guy in handcuffs. Unfortunately, in my effort to get out of the car, I had kind of torn the place up. OK, I had <u>really</u> torn the place up. I don't know who was more surprised by what the inside of the car looked like- Trooper Hayden, the bad guy, or me. Let's just say that that was the last time Trooper Hayden forgot to roll down his window!

When I was about 10 years old (which is very old in doggy years), Trooper Hayden got promoted to Sergeant. I was beginning to slow down a bit and my old hips were really starting to bother me. The decision was made for me to retire. I was NOT happy. Whenever my human put his uniform on, I would get all excited and race to the door. Sometimes, I would sit by his police car and just look at him. I knew that I was not a young pup anymore, but I still wanted to do my job. I think my human knew I was a little mad at him whenever he went to work without me.

**That is me on the right with my furry sidekick, Shadow.**

Being home all the time had its advantages, though. I got to run and play with the kids more and sleep whenever I wanted to. I also got to hang out with my favorite human on his days off. One of the things I liked to do the most with him was to chase after golf balls that he hit into the woods! I could still use some of my training to do that. As I got older, I did less running after the kids and balls- and a lot more sleeping.

When I was 14 years old, it really hurt me to get up and move around at all. I had lived a great life. I had more doggy adventures than most other dogs I knew! I was in a family that loved and included me in everything. My humans knew I was suffering a lot and the decision was made to put me to rest. My whole family cried. Right up until the end, I stayed strong. I wanted to make sure they were going to be all right- and I still watch over them today. They don't know it, but I do. That will be our little secret, though.

## About the Author:

Jen Deering is the daughter of Maine State Trooper (and later Lieutenant) Dennis Hayden. She grew up with Skipper as her playmate and protector. They played endless games of fetch and spent lots of time running around together. She always felt safe when she was home alone with him because no one would dare mess with Skipper (though secretly, he was a big wimp when it came to thunderstorms). More importantly, she knew he always had her dad's back. Skipper was very much a part of happy memories growing up. To this day, Jen cannot see a blue racquetball (his favorite ball to play fetch with) without thinking of Skipper. The author lives in North Carolina with her husband, Mark, and their three children.

## About the Illustrator:

Sarah Deering is Jen's sister-in-law. She lived in Maine for several years and around the world with her Air Force family. She enjoys drawing, painting, and quilting along with other arts and crafts. She lives in South Carolina with her husband and spends lots of quality time with her two sons, daughters-in-law, grandchildren, cats and dog.

48919080R00019

Made in the USA
Charleston, SC
14 November 2015